A PALACE OF PEARLS

A PALACE OF PEARLS

JANE MILLER

ACKNOWLEDGMENTS
Grateful acknowledgment is made to the editors of the following journals, in
which these poems first appeared:

*Boston Review, Colorado Review, CROWD, The Evansville Review, Electronic
Poetry Review, Fence, Free Verse, Hunger Mountain, Iowa Review, jubilat, Open
City, Pool,* and *Volt,* and in *Poets Against the War* (The Nation Books, 2003).

In #30, weights and measures are from *Islam in Andalus,* revised edition by
Ahmad Thomson and Muhammad 'Ata'ur-Rahim (Ta-Ha Publishers,
London, 1996).

Copper Canyon Press is in residence at Fort Worden State Park in Port
Townsend, Washington, under the auspices of Centrum Foundation.
Centrum is a gathering place for artists and creative thinkers from around
the world, students of all ages and backgrounds, and audiences seeking
extraordinary cultural enrichment.

LIBRARY OF CONGRESS CATALOGING-IN-PUBLICATION DATA

Miller, Jane, 1949–
  A palace of pearls / Jane Miller.
     p. cm.
  ISBN 1-55659-222-1 (pbk. : alk. paper)
  I. Title.
  PS3563.I4116P35 2005
  811'.54--DC22

                              2004018211

COPPER CANYON PRESS
Post Office Box 271
Port Townsend, Washington 98368
www.coppercanyonpress.org

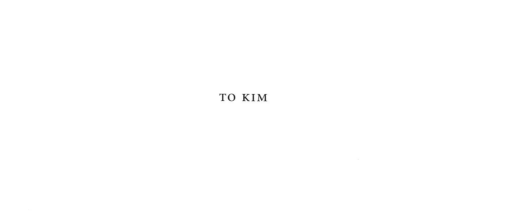

TO KIM

A PALACE OF PEARLS

1

My dead father always makes me think of living

I mean thinking of him dead always moving

across the sky west to east

until the full moon just breaking over

THE HORIZON IS TOTALED BY CLOUDS

2

Lightning lights the moon's shroud

the surface of my body is excited

like sharp stabs of emotion in love

for whose art the sun is god

tonight the senses spring from the soul

as once was thought

a brief release of something unseen then enlightenment

like a gaslamp struck

embarking on a long weekend alone a long week a season a year

another year father trying to pierce the dark

thinking is only ever provisional

this is what I think now that we are both alone

I can't remember enough I make shit up

our time together is now a feeling

and all my thinking about you the flicker of event

the bond of physiognomy a child's distant melodic greeting

by all accounts sketchy lest I make too much of them

lost just in time nothing serious

on my own reconnaissance some admire me some feel sorry

I've spent most of my life

thinking art would make sense of it

A FOOT SOLDIER SEIZED IN SIGHT OF HIS OWN SQUADRON

3

I'm going to see what I can see

whenever it flashes

in the night sky fighter-jets practice

won't their metals attract lightning they appear not to move Jesus

the shadow leaks out of the thing like a fluid but has no relation

to real shadow perfect and perfectly unreflective

is it bloody

I'll call it an accident

that way there can be no relief no foreboding all event

NO ONE WILL BE RESPONSIBLE LEAST OF ALL

4

Do you know how long it has been since a moral choice presented itself

and the wrong choice was made

not two minutes

why is it not quiet between lightning and thunder as if someone

were asking

do you have other articulable feelings   if so express them now

tragedy ensues

with a laser blast from the cockpit

the dangled finger of God makes contact

PLEASE CALL FOR SEVERAL HUNDRED THOUSAND PHYSICIANS

QUICKLY

5

The jumping cholla detaches a finger of stem covered in barbed sheath

that helps the stem stick

rather than fall from the victim

the stem must be withdrawn carefully

like the point of an arrow or fishhook

in the reverse curve of its prick

the cholla flowers open in June late in the evening

wither by morning

its new fruit forms a chain with the older above it

deer and javelina soundlessly brave human habitats in a dry year

a single cholla twelve feet and almost as wide in moonlight is terrifying

I've done nothing to deserve good luck with them

my yard is full of such species

common to the northernmost range of Mexican highlands

and southernmost Rocky Mountain chain

the sharp stab of emotion I feel is exactly nothing compared

to what I have seen coming from them

AS THEY MOVE ABOUT THE INTESTINES OF MY BACKYARD

6

I've tried to write when I haven't been emotionally crippled

it seems there is no right world for it

I have been a coward

I said no when I could have said yes

perhaps it's as simple as everyone learning to read and write

this is a sinister time for the country

dark political plots

the poets have become the asses of the aristocrats

WE HAVE OUR SECRETS

7

Harmony in music is relatively young a few centuries

before that there was no tone

perfection now needs to be more complicated

fliers level the enemy in advance of ground troops

they know nothing of the permanent reprieve of uncertainty

they have their orders

THE THEME OF THE HERO BROUGHT LOW

8

Devoting themselves to the shadowy figure

Goya and Caravaggio deracinated art history

were it not for reality they would be forgotten

the world filtered through obsession and emotion has failed

imaginations have failed to shoot blanks

now Caravaggio has only the bulb of moonlight over his head

and the severed heads of his paintings

I will try to fill in the exposition

I know that has become terribly important

THE LAST DAYS OF AND SO ON

9

Deaf Goya Goya with migraines Goya painting by torchlight

the decrepit old Goya besieged by shadows

Goya in a black mantilla

Goya and failure

grotesque bulbous nose

gargantuan in crepuscular light

Goya painting wearing a metal wreath of candles on his huge head

THE NATURAL LIGHT OF THE NIGHT

CARAVAGGIO THE BULL AND GOYA THE DARK HORSE

What idiot sits in a metal chair by a tin fence

when the storm commences the mountains disappear

in a cloud of clouds the monsters reappear

the result is a remarkably diverse array of desert life

yellow rainlilies for one example

like all pleasures sleep has become a passion

of my father's I remember we would live for these rains

years ago in Spain we'd walk into Alayor

in a downpour the old women under the shades

in dresses and black scarves would not lift one dark eyebrow

from their lacework not so much as a lisp of Catalonian greeting

and why be obliged with Franco not yet dead long enough

there was plenty of talk of how he'd murdered

Lorca among many others by ordering soldiers

to shoot point-blank at their enemy on a back road at dawn

in the presence of their Lord

and the enemies many of them servants of culture set off

MORE OR LESS ON A FOOL'S JOURNEY

12

Inside the storm is like a long train ride

unable to afford a better class

you sit awake all night in a chair

time to time you make your way to the club car

then back to your dream

on on the train plunges maybe you hear music

the train would be headed for a beach town

or the signature nightmare of your people

a shower of darkness

these are extraordinary times

the Inquisition is a clusterfuck of the inner ear

ONE SHOULD NOT STAND IN FOR SOMEONE ELSE UNLESS

THE CHOICE IS CLEAR

13

My girlfriend visits Naples

every bus ride she's shaken down for money

men rub against her beautiful thighs

and if she turns away for five minutes her bags are gone

this bullshit kills me

these fucking Italians

think they can get away with murder

this is how terrifying people can start

to sound when things become personal

crossing the street is another nightmare

traffic never stops you take your life in your hands

IN THE SOUTH THEY WILL KILL FOR A POMEGRANATE

14

Was my best self the painter of my youth

a pretty lousy untrained sensibility

a couple dozen naked figures materialized

in the rain forests of northern California

in an upstairs room what's her name

and what's her name posing for free

I wasn't a good person I cheated on my boyfriend

I lied to my parents saying I was married

I loved someone who was herself

married minor offenses of the bourgeoisie

I skipped school I grew pot

it rained and rained it was unbelievable

TO FELL THE PRECIOUS REDWOOD

TO LIVE IN A REDWOOD HOUSE

15

What is it about Americans

we bully the first people we meet

whole villages of Pima Indians

moved into saguaro forests every June

with long picking sticks they poke the green fruit

they scoop out the pulp

and toss the star-shaped rind down to inspire rain

the innards ripen to iodine-red centers and tiny black seeds

they're made into syrup and jam and pressed into cakes for later

should they need to be shared with manbeasts like us

our prophecy has been written by Shakespeare

you'll be rotten ere you be half ripe

the long picking sticks are made by tying their ribs together

WHEN THE SOFT FLESH FALLS OFF THE FALLEN GIANTS

16

When Caravaggio loses ten *scudi* in a tennis match

with a young man from Turin

they commence beating each other

first with their racquets and later with swords

Caravaggio himself severely wounded attempts to castrate Ranuccio

wounding him in the thigh

and when Ranuccio dies

Caravaggio escapes for a time protected in Naples

if caught he will be decapitated

a capital sentence over his head

finds himself in the throes of painting

The Seven Acts of Mercy from Matthew

For I was hungry and ye gave me meat

I was thirsty and ye gave me drink

I was a stranger and ye took me in

Naked and ye clothed me

I was sick

and ye visited me

I was in prison and ye came unto me

on the right a corpse is carried out of the picture

burying the dead being the final kindness

Caravaggio's thinking he's to be reprieved he's to be forgiven here tragedy superannuates religion

hastening to the beach to board a ship for Rome

for Pope Pius' pardon

he's abandoned at thirty-eight

as the vessel with all his belongings

leaves without him

he runs along the wharf in the heat to catch sight

of the disappearing ship falls ill and is given shelter

all told for less than a day

DEAD THE FEATURES OF THE SICK MAN ARE BARELY VISIBLE

17

The ancient Greek baby sent forth

feet pierced by metal pins

to die on a mountainside

saved by shepherds   raised in glory

an infamous story the plot consists

not of actions Oedipus is fated to perform

but of actions he takes to discover his fate

his public vigorous inquiry

into his father's murder

reveals the man who blocks his path

and whom he slays becomes in truth

his own father more horrors that beggar description

are to be found unbeknownst beds his mother etc.

the innocent sufferer how can that be

JUST MY FATHER IS NOT MY FATHER ANYMORE

18

I'm dreaming your dream

when you were unconscious

and I had to prop you in a wheelchair

and push you across a hotel lobby

dense with insomniacs gesturing

in a cave of neon light the narrative of their lives

coinage they are occasionally repaid

from a slot machine in Vegas

a vague sense of having done something

without remembering details they pull

down and down no night no day

they stop for coffee a smoke and a bite

trying to turn you around to get out

of the empty elevator I've gone up

maybe a hundred maybe a few

hundred flights it seems our floor is missing

we need to regroup except that one of us

is indisposed as your leader I feel responsible

for this delay in our arrival

I will the action forward I find your proper bed

I ice your face I cover your body

then I allow myself to think

of my own needs my room service

my damp fries

finally I'm alone with the television as you are

I remind myself in the least

frightening way possible coming out

of anesthesia to your next medication

a heavily brocaded bedspread and drapes

drawn to keep out the light and the mountain range

which now that I am peeking seem to be closer

a glance inward at the set

provides a snapshot of male adult soldiers

in full battle regalia leveling artillery fire

at rock-throwing children I must be mistaken

I must be tired I must be lonely with you

in an otherworldly sleep the gods had given them the Nile

it was only the foreigners the strangers who needed rain

it's plain how many purely practical duties I could attend

wash you for example offer a prayer

for a time wholly being in the service of

trees and pasture and the home of lions antelope and sheep

THOSE STRANGERS SEEMED FAR AWAY AND HARMLESS

19

Wherever they fell their bodies were buried

the custom was to sit down to one's drink

of an evening which was often incomplete

without a fight or a visit to a brothel

one can still see a girl astride a customer

or down on him in a pleasure bed

more likely than not she was a slave

to lava and volcanic mud hardened

into something as accurate as a sculptor's mold

such that she lives in a death throe

preserved by what destroyed her

civilization being that stage of development

at which writing

and the keeping of written records

is attained a deluxe resort on the Bay of Naples

men bathed in gossip by teenagers

the last days of Pompeii

a catchphrase of any collector

of seashells of musical instruments

and art an angel warming his feet on the mantel

all buried within twenty-four hours

the likes of which ought not to be heard from again

unless it be magic that speaks to us trembling from the next room

of the destruction to come courtesy of

A PATRON WHO HAS PAID TO BE AMUSED

20

In the atrium an opening admits

not only light but also rain

to be caught in a basin set into the floor

on the edge of which is a marble channel

so the rain passes into a cistern nearby

a fountain nymph stands spouting into a marble bowl

to complete the harmony

the substratum of all things which exists only potentially

and upon which form acts to produce realities

surrounds the atrium in the living

shape of four columns of tufa composed

of small nothings from springs and streams

like an arcadian poem built of water

from water to water standing in the vibration

of this splendid house of noble proportion

with the light flooding the atrium one barely sees

the devastation begin at ten o'clock

a plug of lava bottling the cone blows skyward

rock loosens and plummets back into the crater

blocked gas forces through ever more

violently the eruption shakes the mountain

and a rain of ash blacks out the sun

those who are free to run die

outside prisoners and dogs inside

how paltry is metaphor

compared to the sublime city

in ruins imagination repairs

when I was a young woman

and left my father's house forever

there was no way of knowing then

I'd never have children

what is it that may be gleaned

from life in earlier times that life was

short wretched hungry and brutal that people

sought after pleasure that after crisis

there was lamentation and healing there were progeny

there was a future it is still there

a stillness as if one were awaiting

a diagnosis that a civilization given us by gods

and taken away by men this time

will be unrecoverable one will long for the familiar

plunder of shrines and transfer of silver and gold the clanging metals

of the prison cell the cries of an infant of an evening

THE FULL PALE MOON RISING IN LAVENDER SKY

21

You set the net so you don't get bitten

you go to bed you photograph and send this image

ten thousand miles a minute

in an act of intimacy

your face is resolute when I view it

you will have conquered the mosquitoes

at a cost of mild claustrophobia

and I see that you

miss me I remember the sleep you are setting off toward

under that net

as we so often left the hard mineral world

together in the desert

for a radiance peopled by innumerable tiny cherubs' heads

what happens to angels

is that they get younger until they disappear

the man in bed does not look well in Goya's work

by the side of the bed there is a priest holding a figurine of Christ

whose tiny wooden arm flings a rain of blood across the dying man

I mean no disrespect but in the painting

the blessed and horrible miracle

is more or less the imagination of the painter

there is only death

and the ghouls hanging around Christ

Christ the priest and the dying guy

are dead with the Catholic faith of Old Spain

here where I sit confounded by it

of what value is

my poem my feeling for life my distinctions

and comparisons full of myself as if I were

a priest or philosopher born to think across this water

separating us during which time

people are cut they're frightened

they want to know why they want to know

where they are dying well aware

it is not in this poem

one of them holds her heart while her lungs fill with water

she's old in a moment her face is soft her hair is white

she always wanted to die in her own bed

the imagination is suspect it may or may not let her

when I saw her for the last time

she told me to do whatever I wanted

and to enjoy it and it was all the more poignant

with my old mother standing by waiting her turn

when we were alone again it was clear

my mother was thinking of her friend

she went to shut the blinds at dusk

and when I said I'd like to watch

the sky darken said I don't know you

really since you left home so early

I'd wanted another glimpse of palms

my mother wasn't interested turned inward

she is more real than ever who may fall over somewhere

while I am composing myself executing a minor

lugubrious love poem

when five massive ravens set down their weight

five black oily heavy

otherworldly creatures as if I am dead meat

I ought not to make comparisons

every dying bloom is not a toppled head

humanity escapes naturally through a fine net of sunlight

I THINK IT IS A LOVELY DAY

22

My darling would rather raise a goose

before she'd cook and eat it

does that mean she would then eat it

is not such ambiguity

a creamy golden cherry blushing

impenetrable all clear juice and perfume

of honeyed lavender Michelangelo's males

don't have more porcelain beauty than my white peach

my beloved can separation return us

our young and lithe marriage our heroics of love

where I pull back the pale green summer coverlet

upon the manner of our incompleteness a blue

that may not exist in nature and a gray too

beyond our understanding but often present

to find willingness and open air and grandeur

as the sun and the moonlight variously play

upon our round bruised bodies and our bruised sharp minds

our hope seems justified but let us not return

to innocence let us come with half-closed eyes

to feel more powerfully actual than merely real

things stomachs taut with sexual thunder rumbling

some moments of some days at home in our own bed

and live the rest of the time in this great rotten country

trying to make sure there is a rest of the world

it's no example to fathom a banquet of fruit

squeezed and dripped nimbly in the sealed wild

mood of eager mind my darling loves me

unaccountably despite my wasting her time

in this poem while she's hard at work in the real world

of Rome and I'm at home excoriating

a surface a small matter never mind it feels

like my own skin unheroically grating a lime

in God's hands but more ironically than some

Renaissance painters may have thought of the brush

to wit I am as free-spirited as any Roman

thinking about the surface as it reflects the depths

but history is the last thing poems should tell

and stories next to last so poetry is all

a scent of berry like a splash of destiny

which hints at the best of life and after its small

thrill passes like a small lost civilization

it can be solace and sadness as well

no matter how long I write how ill or well

the story say of a lost civilization

or that we might be last of the generations

the poem restores nothing

blueberries limes peaches my love zero

why then is the poet

the last to see as a god

that Earth from the heavens is radiant fruit

CHERRIES BLUEBERRIES WHITE PEACHES AND LIMES

23

The miller is charged to utter a prayer

when wheat and barley flour are ground

bulls and rams both milk and barley fed are sacrificed

the thighs being the prime cut

for this or that god the King eats

a scrap from the golden plate

then the tail goes to the metallurgist

the breast to the goldsmith

and the ribs to the weaver

the priest shall mix wine and good oil

he shall smear it on the door sockets of the gate to the sanctuary

the door shall not be shut

the first watch of the night shall prepare the golden tray

one starts the day thinking of marriage

and ends the day thinking of war

each chariot has a driver and a soldier

a battle-ax and a quiver of spears

after the running and shouting

if there is nothing

is there peace and quiet

the days are long in the desert

not much happens quickly

the most beautiful and well-built young men

have bowls put before them

of honeyed cream and black figs of a violet

less dark green than eggplant skin

and more black than blue and sweeter

than milk for the sacrifice

and after such wonder

that there is a world at all

the scribe has to send the police

TO DRAG RECRUITS FROM THEIR FAMILIES

24

The generally tender cuts of meat in the back of the animal

are forbidden by Jewish law such law

also forbids the consumption of the sciatic nerve

giving rise to long-stewed pot roasts of the forequarter

and that other classic forcemeat gefilte fish such humble meals

as meatballs could be prepared ahead and served

cold on the Sabbath during the trials of the Inquisition

the preparation of albóndigas was presented as evidence

of secret Jewish practice the vast majority having long since fled

only Jews who remained in Spain

and converted to Catholicism

were put to trial rank justice if you will

that the reader may be more justly occasioned

to make inquisition of the truth on the operating table

before the membrane between waking and sleeping is cut

by drugs the surgeon's fine straight teeth appear

like distant white cliffs where I am to be welcomed

as someone who can finally walk

to safety notwithstanding I am not one of the ones

who has chosen to leave nor am I willing

to stay behind as conditions worsen naturally there

is every difference in the world now versus then

with the divine intervention of science

as a way out rather than take what is coming

and I make no case whatever

for bravery it actually became all about my mother

and country in the sense of what one inherits

when there is no choice what one can choose

as a cripple for months I became obsessed

lest I judge those who converted rather than flee

feeling sorry for myself despite what I understood

must be real torture the pain of persecution for no reason

I knew my circumstance to be fundamentally different

yet I remained woefully who I was

having no practice no agency no law

I thought of truth as accessible with my nerves

make as speedy an Inquisition as thou canst into thy own state

O my master I get lucky the white cliffs fade

the room feels positively medieval do I observe

on the white bloodied apron the butcher wipe his knife

determinedly I hang from the meathook where is my mother

shouting from telling me to bring the hose to do some watering

with everything so dry I hear them hosing down the charnel house

when I awake I am walked out of the hospital the prodigal Jew

ON QUIVERING BONES IT MAKES A RINGING OF BELLS

25

A distant engine cranks choking dies refires

sputters revs and finally urges a fully loaded

tools a-jangling Chevy pickup into backing up kicking up

chipped rock and gravel ground to neat shards of old road

of the New West bass notes of mourning

doves *coo coo   coo coo* a disappointing dry wind

a backyard's cache of clinking aluminum

beach chairs toppled metal garbage cans recycled sized

glassware wind plays whistling with

a muffled lumbering garbage truck mounting

a dull shriek shrill whine and grind before rewinding in ever lessening

grunts squeals brakes and concatenating short and long bleats

climbing the hill religiously Tuesdays cranking the dogs into an orgy

of yelps and snaps and growls and fits mercifully

man's *hey come* from a window softens the suffering

amen the singing fires again neighborly regular

irregular rhythms reality's small change

changes one day when one is living

alone too long the mind is excited it begins to hear

the thinking in the singing what music is that

as outside as a suburb or is

the last trash truck with the gaping caul

speaking in tongues the background sounds

that are in here hymns

and other songs of devotion the heart pauses to coordinate

its pumping now the great singing of rounds

to let blood into the heart's chambers

the valve folds gracefully Negro songs and spirituals

out-of-the-way ballads and folk songs too

when the heart pumps blood forward

the valve fills and slams closed Christmas songs and carols

under the pressure Gilbert and Sullivan mustn't tear or leak

patriotic songs for three billion times

lullabies

THE WHOLE FAMILY WILL ENJOY SINGING IN FELLOWSHIP

AROUND A PIANO

26

Beautiful pneumatic local light purples

we have come to summer dusk

clouds gather and lower and damp down and down

in full bloom a monsoon is not yet loosed

gray violets gray light into gray darkness

now it is starless and fatherless the thunder jackhammers

the surrounding mountains finally drop

their load of boulders on the little red and green bulbs of the town

like flashcubes the blue lights of the houses go out

power fails miserably

out marches the resistance army of candles and flashlights

the pounding courses through the body something mighty

I have eaten the little fear worm in the tequila

the Gila monster is at the front and back doors

when I feel for my bed I fear the hypodermic fang

of the diamondback snake

scrub pines are raked up by what

I'm throwing up I've eaten the cold compress

choosing the vantage of the gods

has made enemies of us

the beauty of the storm is misbegotten

it's blown up in our faces

the poem itself

becomes prohibitive one must hire a private car or walk

ONE MUSTN'T TAKE PUBLIC TRANSPORT DURING A WAR

27

The passing years are not numbered

once to express myself

twice out of necessity

three times to pass on a tradition

four times for love

the cycle simply repeats

once for peace

twice for condolence

three times with our backs to the steepest mountain

four dwelling within ourselves

with seeming variation

once in the old world

twice on public lands

three times on a reservation

four times in heaven

auspicious days are determined

once supporting the terraces with stone walls

twice with the theater blacked out

three times to be able to see my father

four times by scorpion

when measurements are taken of our bodies

once with the pathetic little notebook

twice in an ambulance

three times by word association

four by planting sunflowers

and multiplied for the dimensions of our houses

once during an orgasm

twice looking southward

three times without refrigeration

they're adorned with intricate offerings

once lights come and go in the night sky

twice with a sore right lung

three times the argument turns funny

FOUR TIMES UNTIL THEY FINALLY BLOW AWAY

Dressed as a Moor in curtain and towel and plastered in rice powder

a servant gravely recites a semi-invented tale

The Palace of Pearls of which little is recorded

but much might be imagined

for the delectation of two enthralled brothers

with black shiny hair and white starched blouses

as white as funereal roses and black eyes as black

as a sleeveless summer dress of mourning

for an endless hour in an Andalusian garden

before these well-off kids are called to eat lemony squid

and forced to nap from the heat such that years shall pass thus

before they awaken to a day their Granada is surrounded

by Nationalist soldiers who are sneering at them

saying that those who don't wear uniforms should wear skirts

I imagine at night more bullshit with their short cigars

while they search house to house accusing the one slight man

of contacting Russia and hiding

the radio in his piano a vile invention of armed civil authority

who murder Federico García Lorca

on native soil to this day no one is saying

exactly where exactly by which olive trees

does he fall like a puppet do the Guard piss afterward on the shallow

    grave

there comes a reckoning that it might be a failure

to theorize and anyway what's art

all about if it merely lengthens the shadows

that make the cowards evil and the poet immortal

nevertheless even the lowliest poet

would rather go home

to a meal of fireplace embers than not

go down that deserted road

of red earth and imagine the bloody worst

because necessity dictates one must

BE CAREFUL OF MURDERERS IN A PALACE OF PEARLS

29

Have a real night out have a ride on a Vespa

after the rains have cooled the streets

south of Capitoline Hill into the calm of the Aventine

to the little square of mysterious reliefs and dignified cypresses

dressed in needles of wet light the great fantasist

Piranesi gives you a look through a keyhole to the end of the immediate

avenue of trees at the sudden dome of St. Peter's a mere few meters

      away a marvel

of illusion about which much is written and rehearsed the Church

      being

the quintessential Roman sight to see and be overwhelmed by

the spirit of the unseen as holy men so artists have coaxed substance

out of smoke and mirrors the early painters have had their methods

exposed to explain their proficient copying is really a matter of focusing

a lens on canvas and painting in the lines like a coloring book

come to life long ago from the surface of the chemical sea

light-exposed slimy greens creep upriver

and fringe the gravel of forgotten lakes

the little cells wriggling through dew give way

to an ancient time of redwoods and reptiles

when pollen carries by spore and cone seed

to the marvel of a plant

with a seed in its heart

and its own moisture in a pod

the first simple flower is

a drop of water with a little mercurial voice

and the flowering of color floods the grasses

with its holy holy holy and holy

a veritable rainbow of bright optics

eventually as complex and esoteric

as glitzy and twinkling as the new world's

glass and metal skyscrapers downtown

for now we have only the illusion of being

together since love is evanescent a reflection

Gemini lights in a distant window

you return to me first as an essence

alone in the kitchen

PERFUMED WITH WARM PINEAPPLE

30

There arrive fourteen hundred beasts

and four hundred camels of the Sultan's

with a thousand mules hired for the occasion

at the rate of three *mithqals* a month to convey

six thousand blocks of stone great and small polished or rough

and in the building every third day there are delivered

eleven hundred burdens of lime and gypsum

meantime four thousand columns travel from Rome

nineteen from France

the Emperor of Constantinople presents one hundred and forty

and one thousand and thirteen green and rose marble stones leave

     Carthage and Tunis for good

the remainder are native to Andalusia

as for instance the white marble that grows slowly in Tarragona and

     Almería

and the streaked marble that enlivens the coast

with its uselessness and innocence

until it materializes into great wealth

discord and panic and so forth

it is a wonder

the wonders include two fountains with basins

such that when the Caliph receives the smaller one he fixes on it

twelve figures made in the arsenal of Córdoba

of red gold and pearls one like a lion one an antelope

another a crocodile

opposite an eagle and a dragon

a pigeon a falcon a peacock a hen a cock and a vulture all drenched
         in jewels

together they shoot water out their mouths all praise to Allah

proper Arabic for The One and Only God used by Christians

Allaha in Aramaic the mother tongue of Jesus

and *Eloh-im* in Hebrew

peace be upon Him

Allah does not have a plural or gender

Allah does not have any partner

He does not beget

nor was He begotten

behold The Creator and Sustainer of the universe

and the Extravagance of the Buildings for the Reception of the Court

the Barracks for the Troops

the Pleasure Gardens the Baths and So Forth nearly beyond measure

the total expense for hiring amounts to three thousand *mithqals*

a month for the animals alone

one can only imagine that the price for a single slave or prisoner

ordered in the name of Allah into the heat every day to lift

BEYOND WHAT IS HUMANLY POSSIBLE MUST BE AN

ASTONISHING FIGURE

31

When a monk in Reading in the thirteenth century

with perhaps nothing more at heart

than that he's taken by new greens of late spring rain

takes the lovely folk song "Sumer is icumen in"

and makes of it a charmed harmonic round for four

it's time the dreary organum of the Church's

fourths and fifths hack a last phlegmatic cough

and lay its neck of tremulous chords upon the velvet cushion

of the executioner in a public square and let fly the ax

to the box so that a scandalous squawking can be heard

of squabs being carried across the sooty mist of the marketplace

of the Middle Ages squeezed by their feet by a master

anxious to whack their heads and drain the blood

and live by them as a rough seduction of a tune

is in the wind expressing terror or pity

as obviously as a rank smell of animal liver

it comes in little by little little passages in triple time

until the modal drone falls into a deep sleep

listening to the earliest violin open a wound

when its maker is born one busy fly-riddled morning

into an Italian family giving forth

the moan of an orphan a prelude with a single chord of longing

it is all through romanticism we will hear

the emotion gain and lose hold we will journey inward alone

one of those who have left an unmade bed

and the bright off-beat clang of the polis

for the gash in the cosmos with the wind blowing in

it is dark and we are darker pulled

onto a vast proscenium now so finely tuned

to solace and sickness we dare not move

THE GRAND PIANO CRAMMED INTO OUR EAR

32

We bow our heads

for the ancient draping of the gardenia lei in the hotel lobby

and are relieved of our possessions as per a reminder

that one must enter Paradise a little naked

before being ushered to a bed with a view of the eleventh green

lest there be any misunderstanding as regards the native burial grounds

beneath the eleventh which border the semipermanent

hallucinogenic Pacific we learn that any and every bone

is also a guest of the Ritz-Carlton so to speak and is honored

with a prayer if it washes up and is returned to sacred earth

by the keeper of the culture a gentleman of liquescent eyes

as shiny as the kukui nut rinsed in its own oil and as rare

a species of this tropic as a barrel cactus or the fruit of a prickly pear

on the mainland's used-up United other States

as a god he acknowledges we are here to say goodbye

properly to Earth as a house and a garden

because we ourselves have deplaned way too late in the gargantuan day

to explain wriggling in rented rubber face-to-face

with striped convex-eyed cold-blooded creation

way too late to swim out

with shortness of breath up the deeply guarded secret

which the General of the Great Mother reported to the Duke

and subsequently to the King and the Duke himself repeated

to the King who asked to have the President awakened

only to be told the President had never gone to bed

because as the leader of the free world he must importune

the constituents even unto those of us belatedly

craning our necks under a halo of fronds or falling to our knees

in low cerulean tides that he very much hopes we will have enjoyed

our special evening of roast suckling pig buried in fire

unburied and consumed another century has hurriedly concluded

an enchanted evening meal long into morning

with the rest of the day spent

starving begging and thirsty for many and for some eternity

the beleaguered leader announces it is time for the ceremony

on our Hawaiian honeymoon with other charter members

of Western civilization Japanese and Korean pretenders

and a Cuban queen a very handsome oxymoron

orbited by native surfers groundskeepers chefs

housemaids doormen bellhops and a monk

we all gather at the shore for the single-oared canoe

to glide into its slip without its bronzed sailor

as symbolic of there having been a fair game

played by one side everyone on the team shoots an arrow

and the best each round is counted

so that when they are routed

the ship of their little republic is specially delivered

to the newborn fishermen of the island

and thus is it whispered in the wild ginger

THE ANCESTORS ARE ASLEEP IN A SAFE PLACE

33

The family begins early in a remote spot of the desert

hauls well water

makes a fire of a bundle of mesquite

takes the boiling corn off the fire

grinds it

roasts poblanos

grinds them

gathers more mesquite

kills and plucks and cooks a chicken

checks for scorpions

smells for rain

the day is strangely over by sunset

the next day is virtually the same

carried along by an iridescent spirit

like a hummingbird in a monsoon

I am made to look in on it

I can never stay never finish

all so delicious redolent of effort

a pleasurable melancholy

field of stony soil I return at will

but the visit is always cut short by deft soft hands

going about their fixed business

who've served me I see only now indifferently

appropriately as I excuse myself walking barefoot and shirtless

many miles of tiles from room to room of my modest home

near the end of another summer with its embattled project

the jumpy present sends its insubstantial ambulance

STREAKING TOWARD THE EMERGENCY ROOM OF MY

    EARDRUM

34

The place may be clean and tidy

and have for furniture only a mat

if there are windows if they are large

so much the better if there's a flower

or a picture that's special

if there is a teacher

there may be respite from sorrow

if there is rain remember the occasion

of the double rainbow if there is a marriage

there may be need of a goat

about beauty the old ones could not have foreseen

if there is love

think on these things honey nuts and olives

if they are taken from nature

there will be nothing to behold

nor an eye

a poet will have to sing

of the ineffable as true

to begin with

A PALACE OF PEARLS

CODA

The horizon is totaled by clouds

A foot soldier seized in sight of his own squadron

No one will be responsible least of all

Please call for several hundred thousand physicians quickly

As they move about the intestines of my backyard

We have our secrets

The theme of the hero brought low

The last days of and so on

The natural light of the night

Caravaggio the bull and Goya the dark horse

More or less on a fool's journey

One should not stand in for someone else unless the choice is clear

In the south they will kill for a pomegranate

To fell the precious redwood to live in a redwood house

When the soft flesh falls off the fallen giants

Dead the features of the sick man are barely visible

Just my father is not my father anymore

Those strangers seemed far away and harmless

A patron who has paid to be amused

The full pale moon rising in lavender sky

I think it is a lovely day

Cherries blueberries white peaches and limes

To drag recruits from their families

On quivering bones it makes a ringing of bells

The whole family will enjoy singing in fellowship around a piano

One mustn't take public transport during a war

Four times until they finally blow away

Be careful of murderers in a palace

Perfumed with warm pineapple

Beyond what is humanly possible must be an astonishing figure

The grand piano crammed into our ear

The ancestors are asleep in a safe place

Streaking toward the emergency room of my eardrum

A palace of pearls

From the eighth to the fifteenth century, the southernmost region of Spain sustained one of the most spectacular civilizations in history, the Arab kingdom of al-Andalus, a model of ethnic tolerance in which Christian, Muslim, and Jewish traditions in art, language, science, and agriculture flourished.

Despite the region's relatively peaceful life, periodic invasions and conflict with the Spanish monarchy necessitated fortresses, and abominable demands were placed on slaves to build the structures. The fortress often functioned as a pleasure palace, but it was also a self-contained city, with offices, mosques, garrisons, workshops, baths, and dwellings to serve a whole range of social classes. Grandest among these architectural achievements is the Alhambra, the summer residence of Moorish kings, a door of which is pictured on the cover of this book.

Following the Crusades and the "re-conquest" of Spain by Christians, a church was built on the former site of an Alhambran mosque, and King Ferdinand and Queen Isabella issued the Alhambra Decree, sentencing Jews, who had lived relatively well and peacefully under Moorish law, to religious conversion or death. Legend has it that, more than once, blood flowed from the Alhambra's fountains.

Moorish legends and stories abounded in Andalusia, many of which the young poet Federico García Lorca heard in the early years of the twentieth century while growing up in Granada, a place whose sensuous and earthy heritage has given us, in English, "pomegranate" ("*pomme de Granada*") and "garnet." *A Palace of Pearls* is named after an Andalusian folktale enacted by Lorca's caretaker, dressed as a Moor in curtain and towel and plastered in rice powder, gravely reciting and half inventing — as Lorca's brother remembers it, with both boys making fun of, and being enthralled by, her earnest presentation — "The *Alcàzar* of Pearls."

Jane Miller's earlier collections include *Wherever You Lay Your Head; Memory at These Speeds: New and Selected Poems; The Greater Leisures,* a National Poetry Series selection; and *August Zero,* winner of The Western States Book Award. She is the recipient of a Lila Wallace–Reader's Digest Award, a John Simon Guggenheim Memorial Foundation fellowship, and two National Endowment for the Arts fellowships. She lives in Tucson and is on the faculty of the Creative Writing Program at the University of Arizona.

The Chinese character for poetry is made up of two parts: "word" and "temple." It also serves as pressmark for Copper Canyon Press.

Founded in 1972, Copper Canyon Press remains dedicated to publishing poetry exclusively, from Nobel laureates to new and emerging authors. The Press thrives with the generous patronage of readers, writers, booksellers, librarians, teachers, students, and funders—everyone who shares the conviction that poetry invigorates the language and sharpens our appreciation of the world.

Major funding has been provided by:

The Paul G. Allen Family Foundation
Lannan Foundation
National Endowment for the Arts
The Starbucks Foundation
Washington State Arts Commission

For information and catalogs:

COPPER CANYON PRESS
Post Office Box 271
Port Townsend, Washington 98368
360-385-4925
www.coppercanyonpress.org